Rodgers & Hammerstein *for*
UKULELE

Arranged by Jim Beloff

ISBN 978-1-61780-386-4

WILLIAMSON MUSIC®

A RODGERS AND HAMMERSTEIN COMPANY

www.williamsonmusic.com

EXCLUSIVELY DISTRIBUTED BY

HAL•LEONARD®
CORPORATION

7777 W. BLUEMOUND RD. P.O. BOX 13819 MILWAUKEE, WI 53213

Visit Hal Leonard Online at
www.halleonard.com

All at Once You Love Her

from PIPE DREAM

Lyrics by Oscar Hammerstein II
Music by Richard Rodgers

You like her eyes, you tell her so.

She thinks you're wise and clev - er.

You kiss good - night and then you know

You'll kiss good - night for - ev - er.

You won - der where your heart can go,

Then all at once you know. _____

Do-Re-Mi

from THE SOUND OF MUSIC
Lyrics by Oscar Hammerstein II
Music by Richard Rodgers

Edelweiss

from THE SOUND OF MUSIC

Lyrics by Oscar Hammerstein II
Music by Richard Rodgers

Fan Tan Fannie

from FLOWER DRUM SONG

Lyrics by Oscar Hammerstein II
Music by Richard Rodgers

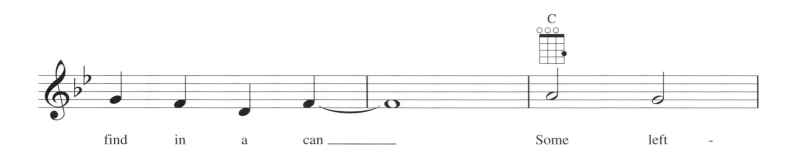

find in a can _____ Some left -

o - vers of Moo Goo Gai Pan. _____

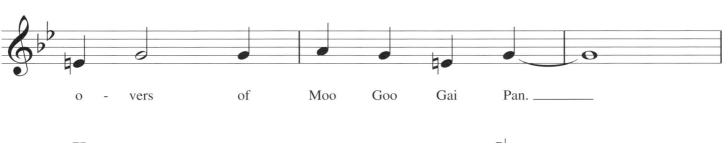

Fan Tan Fan - nie has found a new guy. ___

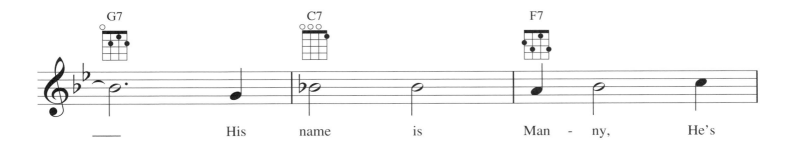

___ His name is Man - ny, He's

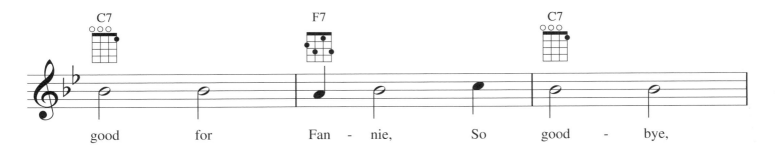

good for Fan - nie, So good - bye,

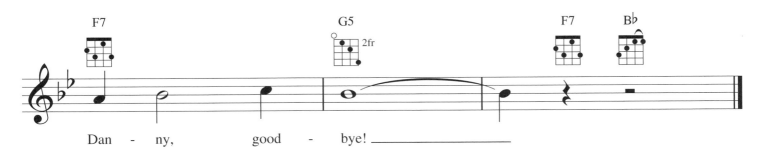

Dan - ny, good - bye! _____

Getting to Know You

from THE KING AND I
Lyrics by Oscar Hammerstein II
Music by Richard Rodgers

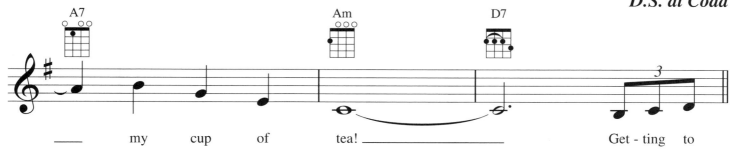

my cup of tea! _____ Get - ting to

Ø Coda

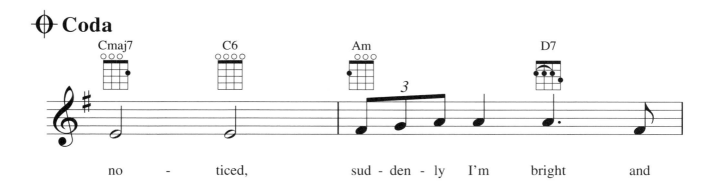

no - ticed, sud - den - ly I'm bright and

breez - y _____ be - cause of all the

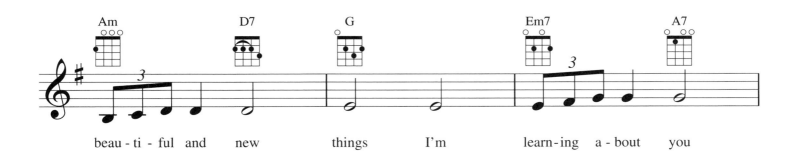

beau - ti - ful and new things I'm learn - ing a - bout you

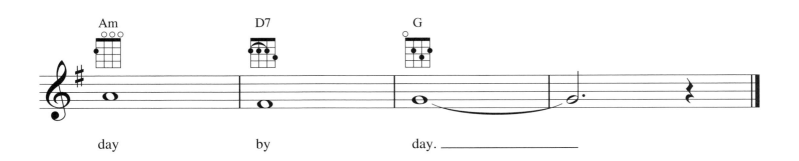

day by day. _____

I Enjoy Being a Girl

from FLOWER DRUM SONG

Lyrics by Oscar Hammerstein II
Music by Richard Rodgers

Impossible

from CINDERELLA

Lyrics by Oscar Hammerstein II
Music by Richard Rodgers

I Have Dreamed

from THE KING AND I
Lyrics by Oscar Hammerstein II
Music by Richard Rodgers

I'm Gonna Wash That Man Right Outa My Hair

from SOUTH PACIFIC

Lyrics by Oscar Hammerstein II
Music by Richard Rodgers

out - a my arms, ___ I'm gon - na wave that man right

out - a my arms, _ And send him on his way. _____

Don't try to patch it up, Tear it up, tear it up! Wash him out, dry him out,

Push him out, fly him out, Can - cel him and let him

go! Yea, sis - ter! ___ I'm gon - na wash that man right

out - a my hair, ___ I'm gon - na wash that man right

If I Loved You

from CAROUSEL

Lyrics by Oscar Hammerstein II
Music by Richard Rodgers

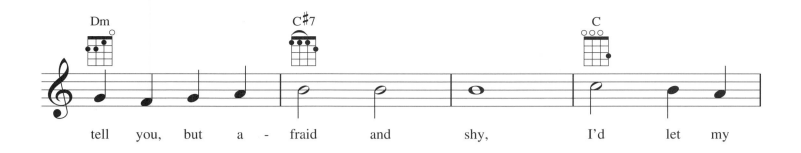

tell   you,   but   a - fraid   and   shy,   I'd   let   my

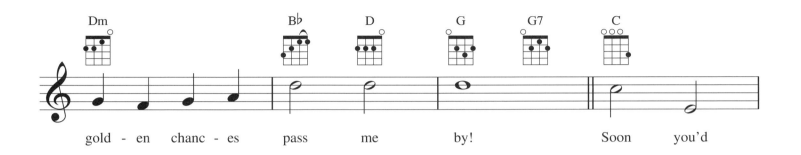

gold - en   chanc - es   pass   me   by!   Soon   you'd

leave   me,   Off ____ you would go ____ in   the   mist   of   day,

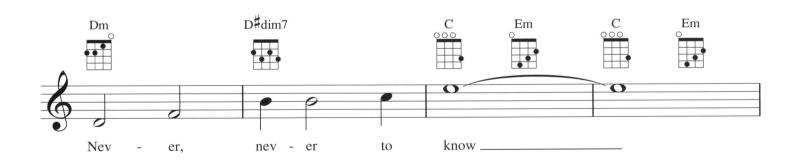

Nev - er,   nev - er   to   know _____

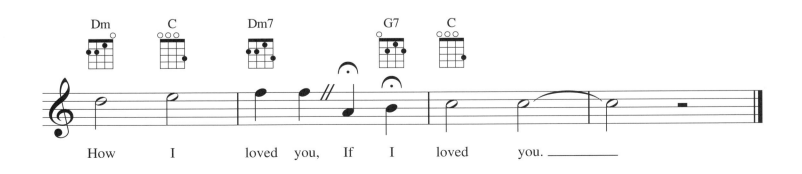

How   I   loved   you,   If   I   loved   you. _____

It Might As Well Be Spring

from STATE FAIR

Lyrics by Oscar Hammerstein II
Music by Richard Rodgers

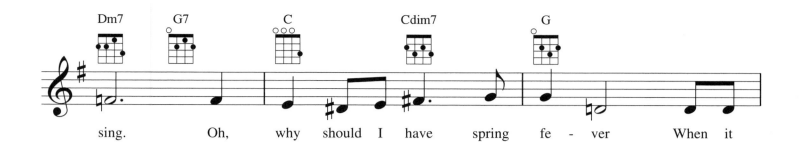

sing.   Oh,   why   should I have   spring   fe - ver   When it

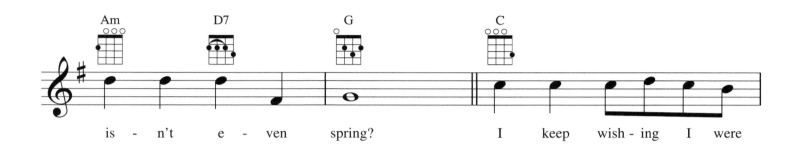

is - n't   e - ven   spring?   I   keep   wish - ing   I were

some - where   else,   walk - ing down a strange, new   street,

Hear - ing words that I have nev - er heard from a { man / girl } I've yet to

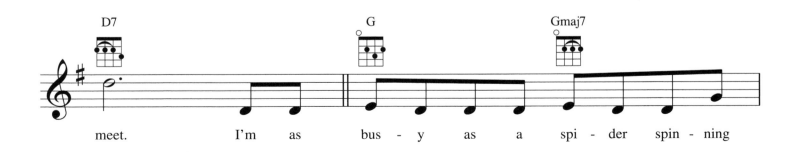

meet.   I'm as bus - y as a spi - der spin - ning

My Favorite Things

from THE SOUND OF MUSIC

Lyrics by Oscar Hammerstein II
Music by Richard Rodgers

First note

Moderately

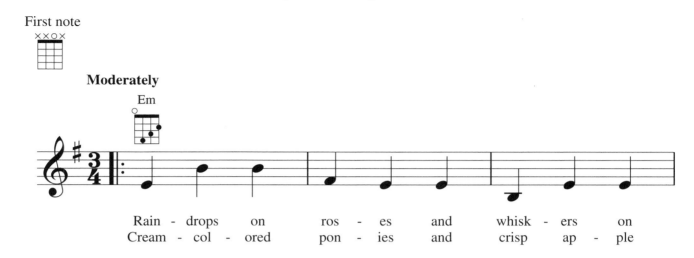

Rain - drops on ros - es and whisk - ers on
Cream - col - ored pon - ies and crisp ap - ple

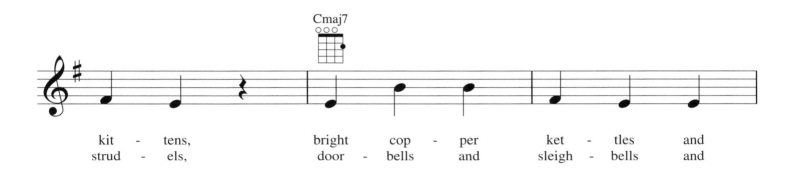

kit - tens, bright cop - per ket - tles and
strud - els, door - bells and sleigh - bells and

warm wool - en mit - tens, brown pa - per
schnitz - el with noo - dles, wild geese that

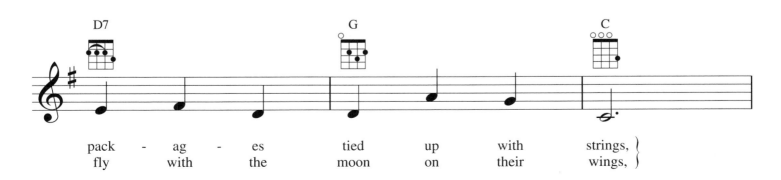

pack - ag - es tied up with strings, }
fly with the moon on their wings, }

these   are   a   few   of   my   fa - vor - ite

things.   fa - vor - ite things.

Girls   in   white   dress - es   with

blue   sat - in   sash - es,   snow - flakes that

stay   on   my   nose   and   eye - lash - es,

sil - ver white win - ters that melt in - to springs,

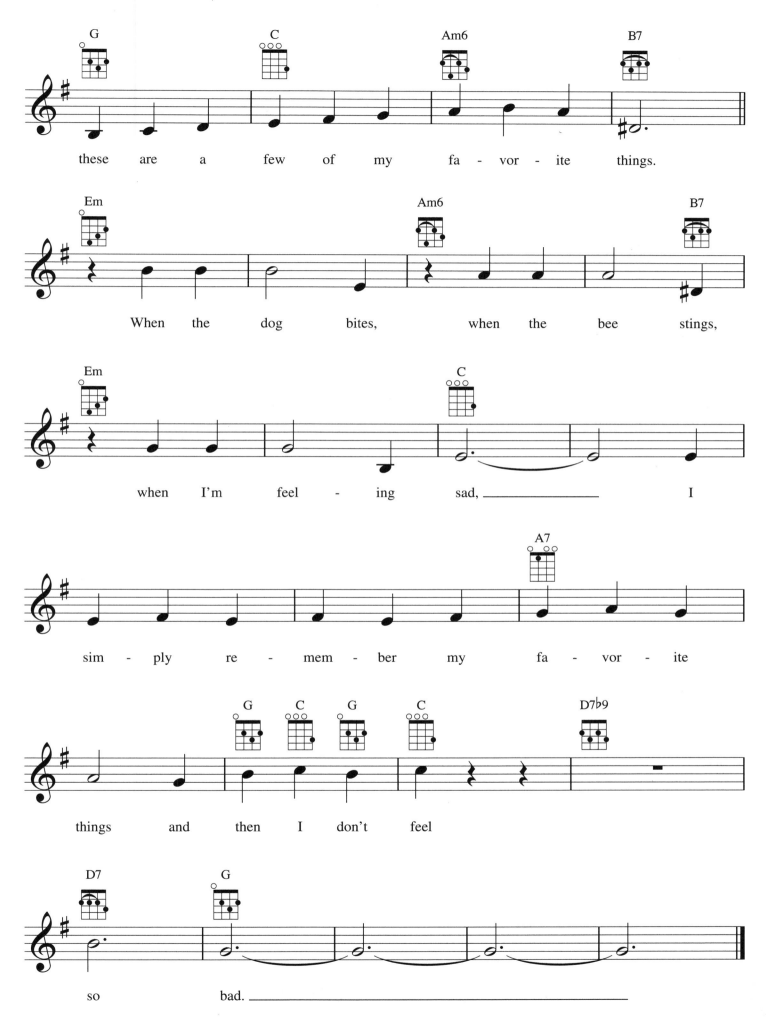

these are a few of my fa - vor - ite things.

When the dog bites, when the bee stings,

when I'm feel - ing sad, _____ I

sim - ply re - mem - ber my fa - vor - ite

things and then I don't feel

so bad. _____

It's a Grand Night for Singing

from STATE FAIR

Lyrics by Oscar Hammerstein II
Music by Richard Rodgers

night   for   sing - ing!   The   stars   are

bright   a - bove, _____   The   earth   is   a -

glow   and   to   add   to   the   show,   I

think   I   am   fall - ing   in   love. _____

Fall - ing,   Fall - ing   in

love. _____

Oh, What a Beautiful Mornin'

from OKLAHOMA!

Lyrics by Oscar Hammerstein II
Music by Richard Rodgers

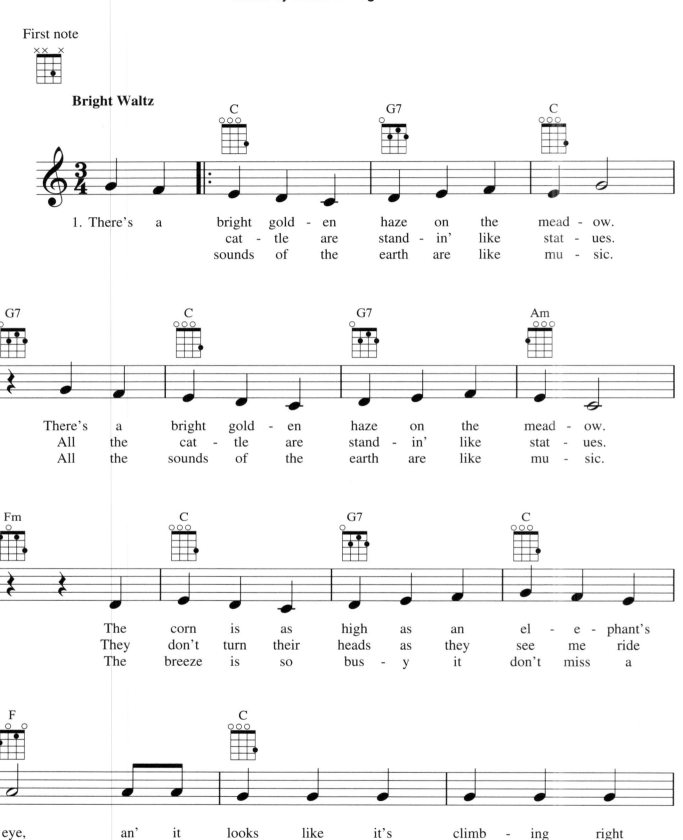

People Will Say We're in Love

from OKLAHOMA!

Lyrics by Oscar Hammerstein II
Music by Richard Rodgers

There Is Nothin' Like a Dame

from SOUTH PACIFIC

Lyrics by Oscar Hammerstein II
Music by Richard Rodgers

We got sun-light on the sand, We got moon-light on the sea, We got man-goes and ba - na - nas You can pick right off a tree, We got vol - ley - ball and ping - pong And a lot of dan - dy games! What ain't we got? We ain't got dames! _____ We get

pack - ag - es from home, We get mov - ies, we get shows, We get
rest - less, we feel blue, We feel lone - ly and, in brief, We feel

speech - es from our skip - per And ad - vice from Tok - yo Rose. We get
ev - 'ry kind of feel - ing but the feel - ing of re - lief. We feel

let - ters doused with per - fume, We get diz - zy from the smell!
hun - gry as the wolf felt When he met Red Rid - ing Hood.

What don't we get? You know darn well!
What don't we feel? We don't feel good!

We got nothin' to put on a clean white suit for.
Lots of things in life are beautiful, but broth - er,

What we need is what there ain't no substi - tute for.
There is one particular thing that is nothin'
whatsoever in any way, shape or form like any oth - er.

There is noth-in' like a dame, _____ Noth-in'
in the world, _____ There is noth-in' you can
name That is an-y-thin' like a

1. dame! _____ We feel
2. dame! _____

There are no books like a dame, _____ Noth-in'
looks like a dame. _____ There are no drinks like a

dame, _____ And noth-in' thinks like a dame. _____

Noth-in' acts like a dame, _____ Or at-

tracts like a dame. _____ There ain't a thing that's

wrong with an - y man here That can't be cured by

put-tin' him near A girl - y, wom-an-ly, fe - male,

fem - i - nine dame! _____

We Kiss in a Shadow

from THE KING AND I
Lyrics by Oscar Hammerstein II
Music by Richard Rodgers

First note

Slowly and tenderly

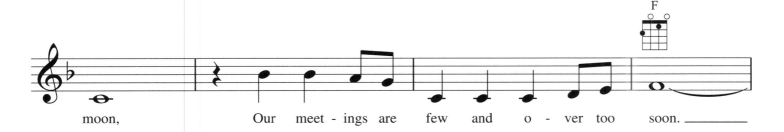

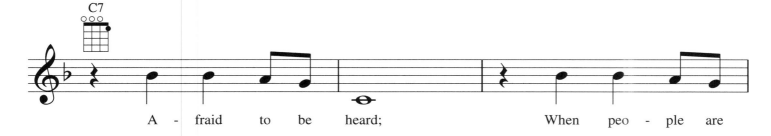

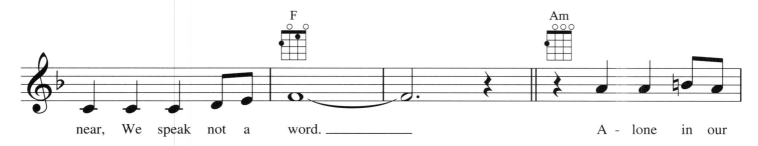

40

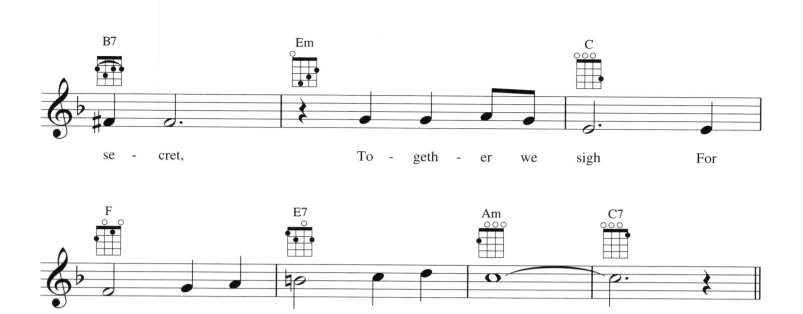

se - cret, To - geth - er we sigh For

one smil - ing day to be free, _____

To kiss in the sun - light And say to the

sky: _____ Be - hold and be - lieve what you

see! _____ Be - hold how my lov - er loves

me! _____

You'll Never Walk Alone

from CAROUSEL

Words by Oscar Hammerstein II
Music by Richard Rodgers

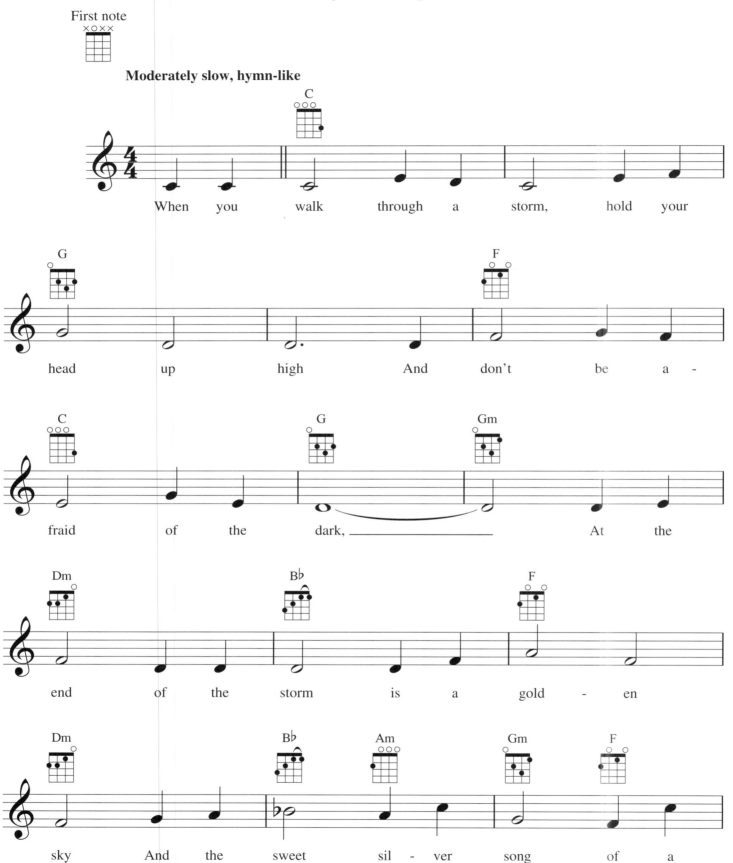

Moderately slow, hymn-like

When you walk through a storm, hold your head up high And don't be a-fraid of the dark, _____ At the end of the storm is a gold - en sky And the sweet sil - ver song of a

Younger Than Springtime

from SOUTH PACIFIC

Lyrics by Oscar Hammerstein II
Music by Richard Rodgers

me. And when your youth and joy in -

vade my arms And fill my heart as

now they do... then... Young - er than Spring - time

am I, Gay - er than laugh - ter am I,

An - gel and lov - er, heav - en and earth am I

with you! _____

The Surrey with the Fringe on Top

from OKLAHOMA!
Lyrics by Oscar Hammerstein II
Music by Richard Rodgers